After the Eye has Eaten

Poems

Tom Kirlin

Poets' Choice Publishing

Copyright © 2023. Poets' Choice Publishing

All rights reserved.

Cover Art: Hazel Kirlin
Cover Design : Kate C. Kirlin
Illustrations : Grace Cavalieri
Graphic Design : Sanket Patel

Printed in the United States of America

Library of Congress Cataloging-in-Publication Data Pending

ISBN 978-1-7371653-1-6

First Edition

Each of the paintings found in this book include the name of the person who owns the painting. They have been reproduced by permission of the artist.

POETS' CHOICE PUBLISHING
AVERY HEIGHTS, SUITE 126
300 BRANDEGEE AVENUE
GROTON, CT 06340
POETS-CHOICE.COM
MARATHONFILM@GMAIL.COM

About the Cover

You may think this cover is the vibrant work of Grace Cavalieri, whose thoughts and paintings appear elsewhere in this book. The cover is, in fact, by Tom Kirlin's mother, Hazel Kirlin, who won a number of awards for her art over the years before her passing at age 102.

The brilliant red, like that found in Cavalieri's work, reminds one of the sun when one has inadvertently looked into that fiery source of life. So it is with Kirlin's poetry, an incandescence which burns long after the eye has taken them in.

The poet takes on eternal themes: love and death, and how both inform our life. And always grief is the underlying source from which the poems rise. This fog dissipates, however, burned off by the rising of an early morning sun.

An unborn child waves from the distance and hovers like an angel throughout Kirlin's landscape. For the works are filled with new love, and the constant effort to carry on, despite grief that threatens so often to wear us down.

These poems are worth reading for the insights and the crafted emotions which reveal the journey of one pilgrim along life's road, a beauty which can sustain us.

Poets' Choice is lucky to have this champion in its stable of fine spirits.

Richard Harteis, Director
Poets' Choice Publishing

For Annie & Kate

TABLE OF CONTENTS

Acknowledgments • **ii**
About the Cover : Richard Harteis • **iii**
Dedication • **v**
Table of Contents • **vi**
Foreword & Art : Grace Cavalieri • **x**
    George Bilgere • **xv**

Poetry I: Familiars • 1

    What Do You Mean? • **3**
    Barberry • **4**
    Kiln • **5**
    Once. Neither • **7**
    Dancing with Circe • **8**
        Unknown Artwork: Acrylic palette on canvas • **9**
    The Mind is Not Here, Not Now • **10**
    Marrow's Bone • **13**
    He Said, She Said • **14**
    Tonight, All I See • **16**
    Olives for Katherine • **18**
    Radishes • **19**
    Uninvited Guest • **20**
        Shirley Brewer • **21**

Poetry II: The Trouble with Ukraine • 23

Italian Triptych • 25
   Unspoken • 25
Via Machiavelli • 27
Ugolino • 29
  I • 29
  II • 31
  III • 33
  IIII • 35
     Katherine Wood • 37
Ars Poetica • 39
Muse and the Gentleman • 40
Solar Plexus • 41
Exposition Croix-rouge • 44
    Natalie Canavor • 45
Paris, The Telenovela • 47
  I.
    Shall We Dance? • 47
    Twilight of the Fauns • 48
    Big Bucks • 49
  II.
    Bold Creatures • 50
    Eats. Shoots. Leaves • 51
  III.
    Dear Diary • 52
    Exist This Passage • 53
    To Origins • 55
    "Arts and Industry" • 57

Poetry III: Unchosen • 59

    After the Eye has Eaten • **61**
    Craigslist • **64**
    Family Tree • **65**
    Killing Days • **67**
    Second Daughter's Birthday • **69**
        Patricia Valdata • **71**
    Green Apples • **72**
    Empty Nest • **76**
    Echo • **78**
    Embrace • **79**
    Christmas • **80**
    Ménage a Trois • **81**
    That Boy, Again? • **82**

Poetry IV: Epilogue • 84

    Book. Released. • **85**
        Caroline Bock • **87**
    Graphic Designer's Biography • **88**
    Artist's Biography • **89**
    Author's Biography • **90**

Foreword & Art

The Eye's Pleasure
Grace Cavalieri

Critics have pointed to many gifts evident in Kirlin's two previous books: *Under the Potato Moon and Enabling Love, A Poetic Tribute* to William Meredith. Now, Poets' Choice Publishing offers us more Kirlin, more wit, elegance, experimentation— and always— more views of this world which could never have been said by another.

Tom Kirlin shapes the filaments of experience into language: romantic, mystical, spiritual, magical— intense poems written with the skill and accuracy of an expert. When we read a book, newly written, nothing like it exists — and this means it's alive with possibilities.

This book is fully alive. In the poem below, ("What Do You Mean?") a relationship is shown, and although we've read accounts of hundreds of relationships, somehow this one surprises and engages. Why? Kirlin knows how to infuse energy into timeless topics.

In this case, the speaker addresses the reader as his lover, through his second wife, who asks: *'What good/ is flesh/for crying?'* Scholars could call this a "volta" stanza. I call it real writing.

What Do You Mean?

In every bed but yours
for years, dear, I looked
for scattered bones.

What good
is flesh
for crying?

A boy, lost—his eyes
shine through mine, rim
the flat sky; flop

> sideways
>
> each time
> you and I
> lie down.

The works in this book combine the experiential and classical. And each poem makes us question whether it's prosody or music which dominates, as each exists, in equal part, forming a rhythmic certainty. From "Twilight of the Fauns," an excerpt shows how naturally language turns to liquid:

> Once beauty deepens, adds
> luster, our minds mark the languor in life. You accept my moon
> -hand, its buff touch, as tides of emotion rise, rush, scrape
> aorta, brush aside collar bone; rinse old fears away.
> True love, I propose, darkens inside as skin glows us into snow.

Relationships make up the spine of many of the book's poems. They ask what we would surrender to get what we want from one another; and how dangerous is the wanting: From "Big Bucks:"

> Still, we belly up to love's oyster bar:
> eat, laugh, despair, feel smug, lisp phrases
> fall drunk under a punk-pink chandelier
> until, elevated floors above, we kiss & rise up
> —your pouty lips spilling coffee from my mug—
> then rush into the anarchy of lust, me tossing tea-cup
>
> pumps into thin air, both of us on a scavenger hunt
> for raw emotions, hoping ancient feelings become
> fresh enough, yet foreign; memorable, untouched
>
> —yes, yes, any strange new nakedness
> that affords *provenance* to the day's
> uncertain birth: to death, to panting sex.

Poetry is the impulse to make everything into a dream and then the poet's job is to turn that into something tangible to include others into his/her nighttime mind. What we look for in art is authenticity; an artist writing from the inimitable; a respect for the reader's intellect. In a world of truncated messages: iPhones, Tik Tok, Instagram, Twitter— we run to poetry for satisfaction.

This is why I like this book so much. It is beautifully complicated with ideas, and esthetics. In some poems the very use of the page's white space makes meaning. Among other dictions, Kirlin knows how best to use the visual to sound and surround pockets of images.

Ars Poetica

    The lurch of beauty

        in the drunk man's

            truth

      arrests

          the sober eye—

        how

    we think

            can so little

      strength

           support

      so much

    surprise?

From the personal to the universal, Kirlin's philosophies speak of the natural mysteries we live with, and how these can be reached with poetry. In the title poem of the book ("After the Eye has Eaten") we hear a lament, a prophesy, a call—to and for our humanness. Poetry redeems and transforms this into a crystalline reality. That's the secret of writing. That's the prize.

> a sudden single singing
> lark struggling to
> gather light across the mind's
> flash-frozen fields.

Grace Cavalieri is Maryland's State Poet Laureate

George Bilgere

I

Familiars

What Do You Mean?

In every bed but yours
for years, dear, I looked

for scattered bones.

What good
is flesh
for crying?

A boy, lost—his eyes
shine through mine, rim

the flat sky—flops
sideways

each time

you and I
lie down.

His shadow
shadows mine.

His unscaled weight
is yours & hers

to keep & carry
—your first wife's—

not mine.

What harm is there in trying?

What else do you
& he & she

keep hiding?

Barberry

I see him run past crimson barberry
I see him hide slight secrets

or peek beneath cherry trees

—a smallish boy, crawling
on hands & knees

he twists though narrow passages
of grief,

this child who
never was

now
forever young:

a love

aborted

gasping
for air

looking for

a body;

some shape

of
understanding.

Kiln

One evening, for her own good reason, she left us
to me, wandered across late evening

thoughts, across lemon grass & aspen
where thrushes preen

and young men sleep
forever. Then, a touch of

… rain. Such plentitude
of solitude

drowned
Keats.

Afterward, at dawn, we talked
of river beds. She climbs

steep cliffs, knees bent
into stirrups. I wait outside

lean on scattered clouds:
sweet-candied dream

windows.

That thunderclap split me.
Sparked muddy waters

—spilling, spits it out.

Now elsewise, dust gathered us
in pitchers; grinds mud to slime

wrestled us to ruin; me in urns—
the moon rocking its writhing body

& we won't let go.

Earth's kiln still slathered
heaps of moonlight, dear

across her shoulders. Still twists time.
But I'd rather life stand bolt upright

all at once, sucks blood
from water, wheels

love to her shape
or yours & mine

—too late.

She & I'd fired blood
to stone

counter
-clock

wise.

Once. Neither

Once, I knew love's callings.
Once, I loved hope deeply.

Once, she & I did familiar things: cooked, ate
made beds, slept, wept, woke to dreams—well & freely.

When summer rose
I seized the day

and pressed it
to a book, openly.

When winter froze

I wrapped light
tight in night's

starched breeze.

I loved that air.
She hated winter.

Now both lie
frozen;

we both
were neither.

Dancing with Circe

Grief is such a greedy whore.

Who taught you that?

She. And he
to grind the river's edge
to lightning strokes

cold as fear
fresh
as regret;

it's undertow

this taste of nothingness

—bent—
a hook

still wet
in the gaping mouth.

*That you and she once tendered love
while he lies cold…*

Not even in the ground!

*…grows intolerable
as…?*

 Faith.

In, what?

Death. That a soul
rests. In peace. Instead

his breath infects.

Roils in me.

The Mind is Not Here, Not Now

You fled? Became this island?

No, no shape divorced
of death arrests
a single word

in horror or joy

or forever forgets
its exact first step

in sand.

That simplest sentence
unwinds its feet
to morning skies

for other eyes.

The same is true
perhaps, of miscarriages

whereby a woman
gains entrance

to a sisterhood
of grieving souls

to the covenant of
good, loving parents.

Yet no ritual warmth
and fewer arms extend

to welcome grieving men
whose partners

end that same most intimate
connection.

Do understand: that's
our frail failing.

I do not seek to take away
what never is or was mine

alone—only to add
equal voice

to public argument,
to stand beside

mother & embryo
yet keep private
what needs be private.

So, yes, for years
I watched suns red-set

on unmoved horizons;
wandered oceans black

with swollen emotions
more pregnant than thirst;

sought birds on wings
—fought creatures fierce—

eager to move
& be moved.

And when winds walked, when waters walked
ashore, or storms burst with words' deceits

with conceits constant as the water's rise & fall
against emotions' shifting walls—

I built & rebuilt ten thousand ocean cities;
tore down them all

without mercy—and partook
of Penelope's intimacies

as if dreaming & not being
equaled being and believing.

Yet never did I once see or admit land and sea and air
can come alive only as seasonal, moveable feasts.

Touch me, then, kiss where you will
for neither am I am rock nor salt, nor wave nor mobius

hanging overhead

nor ship
nor sail nor shore ....

And what? Be wrecked and ruined?

A Flying Dutchman?

Longed for? Sighted
but never
seen?

Marrow's Bone

This much I know:

the throne & innocence
of marriage

was overthrown.

Here, a savage forest grows.

Sorrow lingers
love wanders

where waters once flowed.

Dull as shadows
dear ones
new and old

come and go
in muted tones.

His death
walks on ponds

in me

springs
to winter.

Cracks

the marrow's
bone.

He Said, She Said

Who stammered the first blow?
Did the stonecutter's tongue

strike fool's gold? Why does
love sometimes stutter so?

All fears grow tears
all eyes have ears

No mouth is maiden.

Did a hawk cry out to her raven?
Circle high in the sky, tuck

wings, dive, talons wide
rip the sky's heart open?

All eyes grow tears
all fears have ears

or I am mistaken.

Come, love, come. Unlace
your shame in mine.

Unlace old sorrows.
Kiss this curse away.

No, no mouth be maiden.

Then, let anger be our angel.

No—go live your monkish life
(she said) Spout dreams to scattered

sparrows. I'm too old
to grow green sorrow.

Lie down with me (I plead). Rise
up with suns in no-man's land.

If, by morning light, scorn
grows not ripe, I'll sit tongue-tied

& stare with you at water.
Let reflection be our guide.

Oh, bury that boy! (She screamed)
Feign everyday joy.

Lay siege
to endless sorrow.

I cannot be your sky.
I cannot be your water.

I cannot bear your
yesterday's tomorrows.

Tonight, All I See

is you. Light

lamps the cheek
in oils

bares a shoulder,

turns olive
limb to dusk

as hearts
bend against

spent hours
prone—once

promised
now hollow—

as bodies float
to places

known & not well
known.

Your hand opens
mine to

intimate, aching
shapes

grown inward
& grizzly yet

at great distance.

Striking figures stand
alone, illuminated:

lightning bolts
seize the mind

wielding knives
annealed, shapes

who

scrape away
sinew & bone.

I drift, I know

I don't
I suppose

I never truly
will conjugate

enabling love

—instead
abide inside

beside myself

a split
infinitive:

part adjective
part predicate.

Our hands, conjoined
in marriage mark

land & light:
this waterline

ladened with
missed trust.

Olives for Katherine

Swallowing grief whole, I grow fond of olives
& your taut, raw kisses planted on parched lips
—so unlike her ear lobes, tiny treasure maps.
I'd go diving, daily, for trees: *Sky's the limit.*

Winters, too, taste crisper than her Jonathans—
though once she sprang whole at me, true Italian, all
limb & lineage. Back then, she & I unfurled tongues
mouth-to-mouth, untangling cherry pits as bitten

lips, smitten, pressed harder, darker, deeper
seeking ever sweeter liberties until, at once, she
spit me out, the unripe quince, crying: "Lemon!"

Bitter to her buds, I stood apart, appalled; falling
transfixed—a single finger hushed to lips. Uprooted,
lost in sorrow's thicket, moody as wind, I dried
so quick blackbirds thought me fruitless. By

summer, she & I blossomed to barren, unmarried
cousins. But you & I are Eden-opposites. Not
satisfied with banishment, I often visit a warmer
kitchen; plunge greedy hands in nightfall's half-full

jar of olives, and, stooped in gentlest darkness,
press lips against sorrow's starry basement. Come
love, soft as sin, embrace again the ember hours
wrinkled with grins & pitted hearts. Kiss skin

scarred around a mouth & I will marry each and
every sorrow. I owe you nothing. You owe me nothing
but kindness and, perhaps, grandkids. Eat, sleep, grow
old with me. And kiss. I would be whole again.

Radishes

Gardening at dusk, a penlight salts your tongue
as we turn dirt, pulling dandelion roots & tuber
from spinning Earth—plus one fat mossy clump
of salad greens snatched from the Arctic front

we'll welcome within a week. Now, more than ever
your sideway glance reminds me once we weeded
ground cherries here, this very spot—husks & verbs
of yesteryear—small hand-blown domes seeded

by summer light, saffron globes a child holds
to light to stare through, as we so often do. Soon
we, too, will be pulled from translucent Earth
by roots thin and grey, and planted somewhere to

rot, ceding all fruitful thought. That's why I grow
more crisp than bitter—you, more saucy than hot.

Uninvited Guest

Thanks for penning Cynthia this crisp Christmas note for
the goose dinner. I'll parse her awkward photos of China's

growing infrastructure—glass, steel, flesh, stone—though
most, come winter, I'll mull over Mongolia's frozen roads

& rider, balanced heel to toe; standing on that roan, flying
past her: passionate as snow, slender as a thunderbolt.

'Hooves flying, bootstraps clapping. Lathered in darkness.
Shimmering. Riveting to behold!' she whispered in my ear.

Lust jockeys here. Heated; lean as sorrow. Chaste, I taste
a sharper hunger; wonder: *'Who waits for her at home?'*

Shirley Brewer

II

The Trouble with Ukraine

Italian Triptych

Unspoken

Two young men jump the noon train, Milan to Florence
catching coach. Girlfriend waits one platform below.

Only Mr. Yellow-Pants spoke, elegant arm-strokes
voweling brilliant high notes, heel grinding my big toe

until, windows lowered, he blows red kisses. Every
one misses half-open, pearl lips which Lake Como's

misty fishermen might mistake for storm beacons. So:
she waits, alone, for Mr. Stoic. His feelings never flow;

no *"mio caro"* trills his throat as our train lurches
forward. Buildings fall away. Blue shadows march

in slant light outside *Riggato Emiliano* as flax fields
unevenly unfold, illuminated by the Master's hand.

All around, field hands practice agri-crafts on foot
& tractor. Absent mirrors, a mind blossoms in nature.

Mine sinks back, tastes that girl's alphabet of tears.
Medieval, she tosses me questions from leaden windows;

slashes at love from gunpowder fields, smashes mausoleums;
spouts rage; tears away at basic foundations. One glance

and you blast me back to our first feral, sexy dance
—then Yellow-Pants stands, slaps Dry-Eye's face.

Arms twist, legs brace. Two bulls contest love's brutal
grace & darkest attractions. But no fists clench. None raise.

Exhausted, bodies fall back in seats opposite. Amazed
I later imagine you painting us in Impressionist colors

adding: *A bond breaks, near Amalfi, in a Brecht moment.* But
you didn't; I don't. Scribbled beneath marriage vows

hangs a tarnished plate. Its iconography bears two names
and daughters, plus 30 years—time enough to wake; to speak

ungilded feelings. We know each other's gaze may grow
fearful, frozen; rise up, too, in soiled garments, or lash out

at another's canvas throat. Yet nothing much now needs
painting. The train, stout with silence, blows its iron whistle;

marches us blind through tunnels. I stand, grab luggage &
your hand. Tomorrow, I'll bathe a fevered face in River Arno.

Via Machiavelli

Turning east, we attack *via Niccole Machiavelli*.
The rented Fiat, tires screeching, slays Hondas
Vespas, Ciaos—despotic tin beasts eager to kiss

our dented fender. But off we go, my nubile Red Bull
racing demons—hell-cat cyborgs, engines screaming
each more eager to disrupt the city's civic composure.

Come October? Narrow streets bleed a last lax rover.
Off-season, off-shore, cliffs loft autumn's empty breezes.
Trees snooze; museums close; windows open for a

last long glance at other balconies. Long-suffering
summer changes its olive-green shutters, turns green
-leaf into golds. Blind winter catches a cold. And that

handsome waiter notes your bike's first flat tire. You
smile back, twice, in Italian, and ask for one more fat
pat of butter. I pretended, in English, not to notice.

Later, one park over, I watch a young man grow bolder
circling feminine beauty. He appears, disappears, offers
to escort a girl home. Another—arms, hips, lips flying

open; a sardine of a man—wishes to swim her ocean.
(Those of us less precocious know full-well vehicular
hell awaits such frank displays of drive-by devotion).

That's when an elderly Florentine gentleman approaches.
(City fathers dispatch consigliere to bench foreign notions).
"Passionate imaginations," he intones, *"begets commotion.*

*Gina excites me when she steps half-lit into doorways, arms
akimbo. Every vendor's penny whistle wets, trills. To me
she's part river. We row, never scold; and I'm no scull."*

He goes. You pack. Such confidence feels hopeless, yet I drive
toward some accident, all quite Italian. Seems two musicians
distracted, swerved to better glimpse the girl. Both somersaulted

the Vespa's handlebars, banging curly heads on a curb.
The shorter one rose to curse—having heard you observe:
I've seen Clydesdale horses fall more demurely.

The other, lips curled, spanks a leather case open;
cradles his baby, and, Pan-faced, slashes his blade
across its auburn body, raising spirits with gentle grace

—such a sly centaur. I watch this young goat mount
stoke after stoke until you smile back, warmly. But music
alone never did ignite your ardor. I stroke your left leg;

shout two obscenities & bang that Fiat beast. Tires
smoke, slaying Pan's hope. Even tourists know when
to lock the trunk, shuttering the finest shop's window.

Ugolino

I.

Remembrance hoards her sweetest treasures.
Many may rise up, wrinkled, punctuating friends' faces
who remember nothing

much about us, or recall, on meeting again, we're but cross
-word-puzzles.

Others, knowing even less, tend
to lock themselves inside us—let's say:

as bubbles, or birds in museum cages
who fly away by car or plane in random
sequences.

Names, too, escape:
That old poop!

That's why I need news:
something foreign, something delivered, daily
landing on that familiar doorstep, the brain; or

something completely crumpled—honor & horror will do, though
less forgiven by hearts

than forgotten beauty.

Thus, these travels; foreign trips & domestic visits.
[To do & be beside her, mainly.]
Newspapers & books achieve, for me, much the same.

Take yesterday. *In memoriam*, I picked up
Seamus Heaney's *Field Work*.
Greeted His Grace, Archbishop Roger, Count Ugolino.

Watched the old man wipe away child's hair from a mealy mouth.

Failed, again, miserably, to grimace.

Not him. Me.

Why?
Hard to say.

Perhaps because Old Plagues don't patronize or discriminate?
[They believe.]

Anyway, I'm hanging out all doubt that Modern Arts don't paint Evil clearly, that one's afraid to hang such laundry out in a courtyard.

Yep, just shooting the breeze;
trying to blow the mindful heart.

But first, let's stain the cork & uncork
a mark that marks us all:

Sinners
among
unjust saints.

Aye, that's the stink.
Have a drink.

II.

As far as I can see
madam/sir, salvation rides a red bicycle
every which way:

museum to museum
over cobblestone archways
past sunflower seed days
inside & out

ticking away with monstrous
levity, the way Dali paints hours, giving dark subjects many choices.
Minutes drip, seized with pain; candles curdle into seconds
until odd shapes lie trapped under paint. Emerge.

Today, Great-Great Grandmother Uffizi's gates
stand wide open. Proud lioness of illusion
& delusion, she guards a civilization's dream keepers
of iron fears, a blasphemer full of love & hate.

She opens wide every eye, every emotion; she engages
collects, analyzes, enrages, decimates
images—becomes pregnant, becomes she-wolf
& bearer of museums inside us.

Each, in turn, opens more gates to Ulysses, to Penelope
to Uber, to Lyft, to Molly, etc., etc. Here, visitors discover
Infernos or nirvana or jihad; some seize on bits of unbirthed
homuncular faith.

Such self-guided tours of great castles
coagulate as patrons pay homage
to ages literate & illiterate, happy

they've met celebrities as mad as Aunt Uffizi
who've been raped, cultured or not
by social media, become rancid
bathed in graffiti.

Yet: (weep with me a century
at the feet of one Botticelli

and I will ZIP file you, equally,
a Hieronymus Bosch, besotted; lover
of soiled beauty; icon of demonic levity.)

Still: never will I elevate mine eyes
to celestial ceilings, nor dwell

in Mannered faith, nor sleepwalk
through Facebook nor Rome with castrati,
nor bell awake with feral, fevered gaze

on gilds of gilded zombies
who tear limb from limb
millions of baby sisters
& brothers who suffer, daily.

Can I hear an LOL
or will you sing two Hosannas?

Whatever. Anyway:

III.

War hath poured concrete floors for Modernity, supported neither by Faith, Beauty nor Intelligence, but Fear. That edifice wobbles forth on five codicils:

> 1) Ugolino never ordered the broccoli. Mr. Lino abhors foreplay; can't stomach plant-based foods. He much prefers red meat to filial bonding.

> 2) Photography disrespects divinity. Any Midwesterner can paint a can of tomato soup or beans, repeatedly, and make millions. Moreover, once you cross the East River, who believes your creativity?

> 3) Surrealism and Minimalism define the Atomic Age. Duh! *Reductio ad absurdum.*

> 4) Michelangelo will never master social media. Burnt umber can't mortify flesh the way ones and zeros do. So what if DaVinci mock-painted his family at dinner? Rebuttals just fuck themselves.

> 5) Tribalism breeds Giantism. Not fantasy. Collectively, my tribe is much bigger, stronger and smarter than any other Xenophobic Beasts.

William the Pen best frames art's seminal dilemma:

> *"…what is it in suffering dismays us more:*
> *The capriciousness with which it is dispensed*
> *Or the unflinching way we see it borne?"*

Answers vary. Meredith notes:

> *"We swam in salt*
> *before we crawled to tears."*

To be clear: art vomits horror daily, marches orphans
past open graves, hurls history at caved-in
canvas faces, inspires quaint foreign feelings
in antiseptic robotic places
until the heart throbs
& minds wander
into body/museums
where imagination's images

uncollected, gnaw
on pain's grammar

as works-in-progress
dislodged, often elevate, disgraced

or rest on benches

where vocabularies
build, refreshed

and take shape, tutored
by shapely reflection.

Put differently: I stare
at you, you at me

every single being
leafing through
worlds toward itself

full-on frontal
upside down images:
looking sideways

looking all
ways to tap
roots for patterns, and
 occasionally, meanings.

IV.

German, Dutch, English, French, African
Latin, wandering Jew, Chinese
Islanders, stiff-necked donkeys
beasts of burden, laden brothers

shuffling together, guided
& misguided, focused, unframed
linked by bowel

movements
to heart to hip—we
waltz along galleries
& hallways of history

beneath mobius strips
hung out in outer space
—all of us sisters overhead
& upside down, twisting

turning, twisting again
warmed by solar winds

yet few wanting to join
Elon in that gated community
on Mars, either dead, or just visiting.

Yet—so much Great Art
requires the occasional respite.

Once outside, on *via de Marchi*
an epiphany loiters up:
red hair, pink blouse
full heart, torn jeans,
a drop-dead look-a-like
somewhat blue Seamus Heaney.

But always angelic. After
the big hug, he laughs off
a misspent youth translating
sod into *Beowulf*, love into poetry.

As Klieg lights dim, gradually I
ask the Challenge Question:

*"If Roger, Ugolino & the Uffizi can't channel mortal suffering
into credible belief, what good is death to religious hearts,
infinite thought to brilliant minds, or art to you and me—
given suffering's endless loop, and faith's uncertain liberties?"*

Raising a digging hand
he presses a gnarled finger to my lips
to hush me

rattles his bag of pig bones
and trots back to guard us all—
treasuring above all, nay, eternally
gifts of the mad, glad Aunt Uffizi.

Katherine Wood

Ars Poetica

The lurch of beauty

    in the drunk man's

        truth

     arrests

         the sober eye—

     how

we think

          can so little

    strength

        support

    so much

surprise?

Muse and the Gentleman

To William Meredith
Poet, Pilot, Muse

Touched by illiterate longing, he was like the man
Who could lay a hand across her heart
And you might think this is because his hand
Was familiar, but, truth is, she
Had never had a man who was a friend.

Now he is both afraid of who she is and what
She does, and interested because she says she is
A dancer at a downtown gentlemen's club.

She could touch his arm, intimately,
Or not; he could send flowers, or flowery words
To her hotel room, saying he is coming there, or not.
He thinks he talks too much, sometimes feels unloved.

What do you call this silence, these naked hours
That cry out among us? How do we honor dead poets
Who are not dead—remembered, loved; just not fully enough?

She knew he was neither rich nor poor nor orphaned.
He knew she had a daughter back in Charleston
Whom she bore well before high school graduation.

Online, that summer looking for a hookup, she found
Her heart inside his imagination. His felt full, mine undone.
One wicked wink, a nod, and desires rose for songs unsung.
The brow furrowed, his pen dipped to pages, to tongues.
Words and more words, again and again. Poems. Not sons.

She grew touched that his nose would run, that he savored
Each word's cheerfulness, heroin-addicted to human emotions.

Now hooked, she looked hard on him; he at her. Pretending
To drop a fountain pen, this darling boy glances up
Her formal dress, for art is a leggy dictionary, well-sung.

But what of his legacy? This William the Pen, ever the gentleman?

Solar Plexus

    Word spreads quickly that a small red Cessna iced up
mid-winter & crashed nearby. Minnie Krips wakes up, well, famous.
        It's about time! she notes. For years, she'd offered

        dire, saintly advice about imminent, unusual rural events
and now, suddenly, one accident and neighbor's lives take on
        stunning urgency for believers, & unbelievers, alike.

        By noon, two dozen women had gathered—half-forgotten
wives who've loosened wedding bands, beg Ms. Minnie to press
        forgotten marriage vows to feathered solar plexus & divine.

        My first wife stands first in line: witty, urbane, unsurprised
she sends me, blind, into the darkened room—unsupervised—knowing
        full-well I am "HI," a Hessian Intellectual: unaware, often-times

        of life's soiled garments; untutored, in fact, in events possibly
both treacherous & sublime. Yes, I've carved crop circles in dreams
        with other men's wives; spiraled wildly out of my mind

        falling wet into oat fields. But once inside, Minnie's stern gaze
winnows me down to size. Both windows ice. She, too, seems to crave
        delights of unearthly flight. Whore *and* muse? (How nice.)

        My chest grows tight the more she smiles—and smiles and
smiles. Fat as a barn owl, unflappable as midnight, her eyes & my fears
        quill me tight in her Afghan bedspread. But, being wise, she

        fluffs my shadow into a soft pillow & so begins our flight. Sitting
cross-legged on huge thighs, she sings the White Aria, a swan's unpinioned
        death-song, aching with true delight. Her trumpet notes, plain

        as sight, fall exhausted, so I lean opposite her broad backside.
I tossed her a ten—then, less reluctantly, my gold Waltham watch, my pride
        that first wife engraved one night with a stranger in a motel room

        in honor of *her* maiden flight. Once I gave up on that past
Minnie lost all sight (I pretended to, too, closing one eye) and, abruptly
        her juices ebbed and flowed, double-time. (But not mine.)

"I see you are an archer, or architect." (No, I replied.) *"Well, what are these blue lines? Highways? Did you travel a great distance?"* (Today? Maybe 20 miles.) Perplexed, she shifted here unfathomable

weight twice, once to each side; our bed springs crying aloud as if burned at the stake alive. Facing dark hours, her owl-eyes grew bright. Then: *"Your dim illuminations trouble me,"* she sighed.

"Something terribly wrong, but almost right, seems about to happen. Reveal yourself to me, child! You're...a mystic, a psychic —clairvoyant! Right!?" (How did she know!?)

I smile. (Inside). Sat quiet. Say nothing. *"Okay. When did angels sing you alive? Cause your nape hair to rise? Does your heart still thrum with celestial delight?"* (Long ago, but not twice, for some time.

So, I freeze.) She hammers me twice with that sharp anvil smile knowing I lock fears deep inside; words clank in my throat. Blind, one wing swings behind, seizes a pack of Pall Mall Lights

and decapitating silence, she flicks her Bic before blowing smoke from piercing, addicted, tar-yellow eyes. *(Inhale. Exhale. Inhale. Excite me —I say to myself.)* Hours pass before she offers this sage advice:

"Whatever your flight plans, Sonny, forget distance & time. Seek pattern, shape, rhyme! You've logged far too many out-of-body miles to survive dark skies. What? You expected archangels to drop by?"

I did. As a child, I heard voices, but now saw no guiding light. *"Oh, so today you travelled great distances!"* she cackled, cocking one blind eye at my twisted silence. Trapped, I tossed all fear aside.

"It's fine and dandy" she added, *"to disbelieve gifts as a child but wander too far outside time, and troubled souls like yours & mine —absent bad habits built on feral vows—and few of us survive."*

Her stench burnt my eyes. *Personally, I chose a double—hell a triple—life. Want my advice? Abandon hope. Commit spirit crimes! Fly straight at fear and love. Crash. Burn. Write. Rise. And die!"*

Mad as a hatter & blind, her eyes rolled white—twice. Flecks of gold struck mine. I knew I was going for a long, unfeathered flight. Little more than a vole in her mouth, I bled joy for the ride.

I closed my third eye: imagined her muse—no, nurse—and guide.
She spied every failure, became lover; me complete, contrite. *"Once, I was
an Arapaho bride named Flying Horse, Princess Disney, Lady Undine.*

*"One day, I woke in the backseat of Uncle Charlie's Tahoe Chevy.
He drove to Chicago's south side. I prayed to Gawd I'd make it out alive.
I stayed. Strayed. Found faith in the gutter with itinerant low-lifes."*

She lit a corn-cob pipe. *"Forget, if you can, all your worries. Go
upside. Fight to get inside each insight. Dive. Drive. Makes no difference.
Crash into horizons. Create time by believing in life-decisions.*

Then die." Her smoky mirrors all came alive. *"Speak your craft—
your spirit-life."* "Well," I stumbled, "mine are a bit muddy. Rusty. Quiet.
Sometimes I hear voices, walk about, conjure rhymes."

"Oh, so you're a poet." *(No. Never! I ....)* "Crash and burn!"
she shrieked. So, I kissed those gypsy lips, pitched a last dime & fled that
Waltham wife—fledging a broken-heart, wanton as the brazen skies.

Exposition Croix-rouge

By the time he sits, I'm convinced she's Swiss
or Dutch. Her mascara runs. She'll pay twice for this:
first, to fix lipstick; then, that Hermes neckerchief.

A tailored beauty, measured in means, she leans
tear-stained arms on the tan-suited friend—slightest
of gentlemen, eager to advise, to please, to drop by

for lunch at *Palais des nations*. Devoted to world peace
& culture, he's a perfect specimen of gloved vanity, a muffled
heart-ache, scrubbed; the walking plague, a case of *Coeur fou*.

The scene, too, fits perfectly: peacocks, eye-level, strutting in
front of sunken lunchroom, eyeing half-eaten heart-of-lettuce
sandwiches; knees bent, prancing; bald-eyed. She, seated, not hungry.

Finished at last, I rush a beggar's hard plastic tray past her,
distant neighbors. She, cold-faced, cheeks flushed, gives garlic
tears away, more albino mice fleeing that bare cupboard face.

Strange, how not 60 minutes ago we warmly bumped elbows
beneath a UN mobile—this one, shanks of polished steel adorned
with shoes and prosthetics: dedicated to *enfant amputees*, hanged

in honor of Old-World order, so as to recall war, love, lost memory.
Achille's heel turned his to fear—as her arm did in me, until all *Iliad*
roared in blood-shot ears. Now, no beast nor man nor mating swan

erupts quicker or grows plumper than Jet d'Eau on Ile Rousseau.
Stiff-necked he puffs, erect, expectant of more waters; lifts, untouched
ready to fill, to spill again. Yet it's love's twists rushes the rub: looks
here, breaks there. Clutched, hearts fill. Arms empty? Legs go numb.

Natalie Canavor

Paris, the Telenovela

I.

Shall We Dance?

Thursday evening tired tourists
pretending to be Parisian, eat *pâté*.
Friday, constipated pigeons drop everything.

Saturday, on weekend walks, handbag dogs
trot off to market. Sunday, well-heeled *matrones*
prance that avian dance past piles of *merde de chien*

to shop, kiss coffee, eat baguettes, sip sorrow & sit
sideways between croissant cats, curled quiet in naps
after questionable yawns. Soon, all across France, affection

dies, withered to a dozen cut white roses. Stars, abandoned
sleep on doorsteps, their cellophane wounds wrapped too tight.
Later, neon beggars loiter out. Shadows gather & tearful sirens flash

about in red tumescence; now heathen-tourists stumble out to buy cigarettes
& rainy accents, crying: *Henri! Henri!* All of this helps purchase the night.

Twilight of the Fauns

All Paris loves a charade. I needle Bizet. You slip
into something crepe. Violins stroll odd sentiments away
across a balcony of lights. You shimmer. I stutter & shake

and an ovation of clouds builds south, perfectly on pointe
—lightning legs annealed. *Reminds me of old Africa, you say.*
No, I riposte: Kilimanjaro. Note the tall one's cold shoulder.

Yesterday, *Le Monde* announced no foreign agents practice tricks
in France; terrorists dare not raise a penciled eyebrow, else face,
they say, a massive national revolt. Yet what else but unforgiveable

kisses may the colonized inflict on cruel master? Dance a Can
-Can? Join *Follies Bergère?* Say *Arc d' Triomphe's* a stone clitoris?
Terrorism thrusts upward, its body-politic ever more repugnant;

pregnant. For days, wandering *Champs-Elysees*, unemployed, we
grow into tourists. Terrorists? You gaze into shops, I at windows.
Once bronzed, your scapula's a lion's flank. Once beauty deepens, adds

luster, our minds mark the languor in life: you accept my moon
-hand, its buff touch, and tides of emotion rise, rush, scrape
aorta, brush aside collar bone; rinse old fears away.

True love, I propose, darkens inside as skin glows us into snow.
For, as you once noted: *The gods we believe in, no one truly knows.*
Idolatry, too, falls away, I suppose; levitates bodies, spirits, anyway;

steps far from cul-de-sac cities, past history—skips wax images
& solipsistic ghosts we forged of ourselves; certainly exposes
lactose intolerant old goat eager to join Elon's Martian community.

What's left is a sack of bones. So, as twilight swells, fondling hope;
as cathedrals bell uncertain darkness, I place faith in what gargoyles
know: *Stick out a rough tongue at those manhandling scrimshaw;*
avoid terrorists who loathe pomegranate & onion; never mount goats.

Big Bucks

Sartre, our bellhop, arrives late, antes up big
bucks for a five-star hotel. Its glassy canopy slopes
but feels safe, turns tourists into lightning bugs.

Still, we belly up to love's oyster bar:
eat, laugh, despair, feel smug, lisp phrases
fall drunk under a punk-pink chandelier

until, elevated floors above, we kiss & rise up
—your pouty lips spilling coffee from my mug—
then rush into the anarchy of lust, me tossing tea-cup

pumps into thin air, both of us on a scavenger hunt
for raw emotions, hoping ancient feelings become
fresh enough, yet foreign; memorable, untouched

—yes, yes, any strange new nakedness
that affords *provenance* to the day's
uncertain birth: to death, to panting sex.

But no. Alone, even together, in France, feelings
slip into subway hip-bumps
even though, long ago, we mastered
old age's Stations of the Cross.

Wanderlust on foreign soil never promised much
more than cafes, brunch, two cathedrals, small museums & the slow
hump home on fresh-baked bunions; perhaps, thick hot chocolate
with Ms. Epson, that salty goddess who bubbles
just enough to create scandalous sighs.
She's one *femme fatale* I trust—dirty mind, tart tongue.

Refreshed enough, your legs entwine mine; we soak
up pain anew like a late edition of *Le Monde*
until, flummoxed by ever more cuff buttons, you abandon
my bus and announce: *"Sibylline or Catholic, time's up."*

Rolling over, I nod. Hours grouse brown; odalisque.
Tomorrow may be cloudy, divine, priceless, cold. Sackcloth
and ashes drape the wrinkled spirit, eyeliding all interior horizons.
I imagine dawn, the vineyard: dewy, half-awake, naked. Dangling a leg.
Each second, a grape. Voluptuous.

II.

Bold Creatures

"Noah? Party of two? Reservation for lunch?"
We've come to *Le Carillon*, November 13th
"Follow me." *(Who doesn't enjoy fine dining?)*

"Call me Ishmael, Ahmed, Mohammed
or Dorothy. I'll be your *Maître d'*."
(Garcon pulls back the cane-backed chair.)

"Not to worry, *Madame*. Chef L'Charun
earned three-stars last week. True, he licks himself
and spits—but that's it." (Unfolds large wine sheet.)

"House specialty today—and every day
Praise Allah—*trois* terrorists busting through
swinging doors, or—my favorite—dishwashers

dressed in red crescent sheets, eager to discharge
automatic weapons at citizenry. Dessert? C-4
explosives. With or without whipped cream."

(Lights our candle.) "Allow me, Madame
to remove this *fourchette*. Neither of you or I
wants me to stick it in your husband's neck."

(About the Bordeaux....?) "No monsieur.
Far too messy. Today, you see, I'm wearing
the bespoke cummerbund. My suicide vest."

Eats. Shoots. Leaves

Caliphate sufferings transmogrifies flesh
splattering folk, *al fresco*, on streets & ceilings.
Once squeezed, no trigger, no appetizer, no taste

feels more 3-D than *crème glacee* carts
careening down *Le Carillon's* streets. Cleverly
disguised as calliopes, masked drivers peddle

just one brand of suffering: *"Allah Akbar! Allah Akbar!"*
('Hell hath no fury like belief!' shouts the *Maître d'*
wielding his meat cleaver. 'My Charun's no vegan!')

How else explain turnip-colored blood spurting
stars & roses on so many street corners. *"Je ne suis
Henri! Je suis pas Henri! Je ne suis pas Henri!"*

"Excuse me. Did you just say: 'Nothing compares
to a fine leg?'" Exactly, I reply. Eiffel's Tower's
but a giant iron gam, gartered to a cobbled street.

Comic relief carves a boulevard in painful upheavals
—the time/space continuums less believable once
a patron's flambeed leg is the blue plate special.

Par Example, a plaque about France's upside-down
history led me, yesterday, to an underground museum
filled with skulls, bones, radius, ulna, femurs. Daily

Parisians walk, often without knowledge or empathy
atop an Ossuary. Centuries ago, city fathers exhumed
limestone to erect this metropolis' famed façade:

tall tombstones, aglow, whose holes, plagued, are filled
with fermented bodies. Sommeliers might note: *Acrid. Oaky.*
Not today: *Active Shooter!* Strange, how minds uncork.

One sniff of horror & brains regard skulls as baby dinosaur
eggs—*that's their job, isn't it: to entertain unhappy hearts*
—or scream bloody murder. *Terrorists incite social seizures.*

III.

Dear Diary

Vestibules of breath, fortified
by death, fill, fulfill, violate the chest
with dirt.

Thus, a city shines, dear, yours and mine
blessed to inhale—exhale—youth's

thorny innocence, forever proud
to be crowned at our mother's loins
by birth.

Later, celebrated in marriage, later still, scorned
in divorce, each breath expiring, wedded to death

as we wander into the world.

No Sistine Chapel, yet
nor likely to be; few saints died less
chastened souls. Old walls feel bombed-out.

Still, Da Vinci gilded day-laborers in gold-leaf.
Great-grandfather Cyprien Rouvière
would have none of that.

We kids often watched him spank chickens to bed;
heard him tell stories to Noel, his wife, before "Goodnight.'
I remember him reading us wide-eyed with that nasal accent:

The French? Born peasants. We struggle behind
beasts to become human. Work fields, knowing, if we
don't, we will become what most we fear to believe.

So, teach one other. Scatter seed. Harvest yourself
yearly. Celebrate no god carved in any man's image.
Be the feast. No greater cook can be conceived.

Exit this Passage

Horror & honor roar home, roasting
sorrow from our bones, the 747 spitted
on Clouds of Unknowing.

Vestibules of breath, fortified
by death, enter the chest, full of dirt.
Well…, I guess.

Outside, thick with darkness, skylarks build
bridges across a mystic Atlantic. Surging water gathers
land to light, scatters us again, each wave a sigh.
Complete.

A child's yawn unites us, stranger among strangers
around the carrousel of boredom. Faith, too, in luggage
finally arrives, banging against lost pride—not unlike
little Mona Lisa, her mom's hot pink stickers & ribbons tied
to a suitcase, a tribute to selfies.

Don't you see? you say, Da Vinci's conceit's quite miraculous
by being ordinary—she's hiding missing teeth.
Common vanity mystifies her into a radiant beauty.

Whatever its reason, death never sleeps
like that little girl in… (Need to find
SUV keys. Garage B.)

And here it comes—again. Sunrise. Airborne. Earth
without passport or dreams, just gravity & dirt rising
beneath our feet. Destination? Oval & circular.

Pointless?

But Home. You climb into Wednesday's pajamas.
I read *Le Monde*, count no new bodies. Smell toast, think L'Ossuary.
(No mention of Mohammad, Ahmed. No C. Hebdo. Or Dorothy.)

The trouble with Ukraine, dear, is not suffering.
Old news grows new, repeatedly.

What's missing in suffering is an ending.
No *Dies Irae*.

Suffering neither promises nor contains one.
Only death does.

Here comes that beast, again.

Bombing
toward Kyiv.

To Origins

Parisii Celt, guardian of Seine marshes
viewed its many muddy ditches as but one
troubled mind—smashed, splattered—

and so armed themselves with bridges.
Known as 'kettle people,' these few
Celt kept the barrel-fires burning.

"Welcome," they'd say to equally alarmed
Frank and Norse warrior-husbands. Strange
how easily they & others became civilized

almost: face-to-face with fire-hardened axes
tasting blood, stagnant, in water pail & ale,
more than few remarked, foregoing battle
later, how feigned mercy set the finer table.

Art and Industry

III.

Unchosen

After the Eye has Eaten

the mind.   is a troubled
beast   the brain a whirligig

of odd emotions   cast out
body   blood   fluid

sputum   spit out.
the   hand   a trembling

limp electric prod
waking   touching the dazed face.

cows   crows   eyes   grace
open wide to   shattered shapes

of hope   & loathsome memory.
the soul   empty   as   today

inside the scarecrow   body
bound   to skin & bones;

its epileptic   heart
a   sudden   single singing

lark   struggling   to
gather light   across the mind's

flash-frozen   fields.
(Sky-blazing Vincent
I see I hear   I believe
lighting
bolts

Earth

to fields scorched
in frightful orbit).

Blessed is he
who goes   to war

for words, for images

bleeding in many tongues
dancing   painting   panting

again and again
terrified, bold as any sun

—you, Vincent
freed shape from bone

released
light's

given word

your piety
inflaming Earth.

I never will forget
first blows. You stroked

shape with such firm devotion

turning heads
our hearts

to brotherly
heaven, your wounds

exposed
to blazing worlds,

scattering circled
light: trembling, terrified.

Familiar, unspeakable spaces
opened:
Spoken.

Craigslist

I cannot jog past another porch pick-up
before I come home drunk, with Jesus and a
lamp, walking in someone else's shoes. Last night
Salvador Dali danced backward past me, a bartender.

Slowly, I've lost track of pants, cars, keys, friends
belief. Driven half-mad to sobriety, I've kicked in doors;
a marriage. Bodies pile up—frozen, fixed, asleep—until
starvation wakes to stars, to virgin need. Contempt upholds
a mirror with birds in me; and pity, that shirt I once ironed
in a rented room, flees. Covid, you dog, you slumlord, you whore—
go back to sleep. Or trot next door. Press a primordial pink nose
against another animal handler's keep. Make my days dreary dreams

of faith & binge TV. The horror of it—you possum! Noshing on
garbage lungs. Waddling on raw feet. Fearing want's leprosy.

Family Tree

The spring she stopped loving him, he planted
roses and climbed the cherry tree. Soured by a
squirrel's chatter, dad cherished her beauty above
all others, climbing high as the third-floor balcony.

Nestled inside that crook, master of *prunus avium*
he feasted fat as a cello on its tart red treats
while autumn fiddled with his wounded fantasies.

Yet, to his credit, he never once spit out her scoldings
or blew a single kiss at morning glories, so flushed
in cheek was he, & she, blushed with subtle colors.

Back then, if hearts strayed, vows grew rigid; folks
did little more than raise kids. Bodies cared, yet lay
absent beside each other. Eventually, of course, he
grew into a thorn at her bedside. Because friends and

neighbors do stop by to gossip, grin and dither, one
did ask why she stopped loving him. Mom rightly
offered two good reasons. *First,* she said, *John built
a hog shed years before my country kitchen.* Second

(unsaid) Marian-the-Librarian, frail of stature & spine
proved no easy prey to a mountain wife who felled
her hawk-of-a-husband with one strike, then held
him high for forty years on a strong, bronze arm.

(Fledglings at their knees, we puzzled teens wondered
why she shuddered perceptibly when he unfolded dreams
& slipped a sunburnt hand over her slumped shoulder.)

So, I know, dear: kids are weaned on grief. Her dad
abandoned family—didn't fight cattle ranchers. Fled

instead to Albuquerque. Our dad lost his sister, 1918
influenza; both teens. Parents often blow it. Words
fly about like wounded starlings; fail us, miserably.

But I do love you. And when winter ripens, I'll stand
inside harsh light, equal to this autumn gaze—or
fall away, forgotten. Rotten. Bruised. Not guilty.

Killing Days

For Annie

Nearing 15, she demands a puppy. We keep on
weeding, knowing nothing ripens faster than a
teenager's pouty face. Arching brow, you let her
have it: *"Have you learned nothing of the world's*

cruel ways?" I wipe a dry face. She wails away: *"I
want a puppy. Another Charlie. Unconditional love!"*
You eye the gate, knowing it's my turn. I toss
aside a dozen dead geraniums, keep digging that

awkward way parents have when witnessing love's
disgusted face. *(Best to ignore her)*. Unperturbed, she
blubbers on, hoping a third plea charms me from cold
indifferent ways: *"A puppy would give me such love!"*

You dropped the iron tongue; your maternal gait having
swept you away, I alone face her hail of arrows. Such
have driven armed men half-nuts, or even lame
in battle (think Achilles), for nothing tests a family's

fortress of faith more than a young one's love-wants.
Kin wander off, go to war, marry the wrong spouse,
return prodigal. Call it tribal war or fate: I knew I'd fail
to teach this child to hold a hurtful world to account

if I gave ground. She wiped tears; lay her wish at my feet.
I refused the offering. *"There's an etiquette to pain, missy."*
I began. *"You must..."* But quickly she spurned that
message, twisted away. I took after, insisting my lesson

not be in vain. That's when she spun—and I saw hate
blot her freckle-faced, watched a bawling girl spit one
half-eaten heart at me. Unmoved, I glared back, closed
distance between us & thought Archangel Gabriel screamed:

*"You don't NEED another puppy! You never NEED
anything!"* Fierce incarnate pain burst into flames
as we two stared square inside kin's sacred place—
and just as suddenly she strode off, my mortal enemy.

I crouched under an elm, having played (I thought) a sage
if muttering fool. She vanished. Hours waited. I glanced
at you, drying dishes at an open kitchen window. Your
sigh alone said it all: *"No wonder Jesus never married!"*

And yet we keep faith, and must, in family. We believe in
killing days, in justice owed to Abraham, Isaac, Jack & Ruhu,
Sarah & LaToya: that families must test faith in bonds and
progeny, knowing innocent fantasies must be slaughtered

daily, else growing spirits never will survive or become wise
in a troubled world. We all die, but need not curl up inside
fear's blemished innocence, blaming fate. Today, that girl
a pediatric nurse practitioner, heals kids bawling in pain.

Second Daughter's Birthday

For Kate

Hours later, she wakes the new day, her nymph face
weaving through crowded, common places until
evening invites us in; so we sit, as we must, with
her photogenic friends, in the living room, minutes

before light's screen door whispers a last taffeta sigh.
Time shutters; darkness thickens as we peer out at
the moon's half-crazed face. It's awake, delicate as ever
—a creature overtaken by a rude world's restless wants.

In my dreams, lately, daughter, I imagined you going
away, and tonight, you're off to college. Mom and I
sit shell-shocked on a couch, just this side of
midnight, our stitched-on smiles slightly sideways.

Backs straight, we wait for one promised knock, one
that brings you back with someone just as precious as
when you first arrived: the unexpected moth, who grew
to eat holes in our lives. Now you are going, are gone

and soon will arrive, we trust, with new friends, as
dinner guests—or with gifted child—an Emily, Luke
or John. I suspect we may cry, or not, dazzled by the prize.
For now, I will sit this while, smiling along, and recall

our first wobbly steps as parents, cast in memory's bronze.
Kate, in these loving hours, our fingers cross. We thrust you
out—yes, release you to blind night. May you always rush
toward light, never forgetting darkness; warmed by goodbyes.

Patricia Valdata

Green Apples

To S. L.

Happy Birthday, St. Stephen!

We celebrate
your half-carved life

of bruised cuts
& moon days,

your diabetic agony
running bone deep

as you spiral away
exposing seeds

of starry faith
we brothers

of little faith
circle & uncircle

in our antiseptic hours;
we fraught skeptics

full of mute doubts
& life-scars.

The loving pictures
you've hung for us

in Florence & Madrid
in Wuhan & other spaces

I often visit

or imagine I did

as silences build
anew, sprout anew

in pock-marked horror
across my tongue

as hours drip
—unhosted, sacred seconds—

as months melt away
as years drop away, the way your doubts

did, the longer
you almost lived:

a ruined vessel
rinsed out in Indianapolis,

your body folding in upon
itself, more mud

than white wrinkled linen;
nearly boneless.

My own religious deaths,
fortified by a doubting

name, never truly amounted
to much, yet

your tender presence
elevated it.

A last, fleeting visit offered
another benediction

to our brotherly troubles.
I trimmed your beard,

named hairs upon your head;
dressed you inelegantly

for bed and unfurled
myself around you,

feeling tired, rotund, trite
robust; empty of chest.

Yes, my breath reeked
of rum, but your lungs

rasped acrid; homiletic;
sober, angelic. Dead.

St. Stephen, I pray
you find peace. I pray

suffering exposed
to the core each mystery

that troubled your sleep.
I pray its hidden seeds

help you blow out
the moon's 28

fake candles

—and that you ghost me. Now
may we walk together, wounded

infidels, casting brotherly
shadows across faith's

strange & holy land
blindly feeling

our way toward one
another, touching loving

faces each day with resolute
unresurrected hands

the way I raise mine to you now:
bruised, open; unrhymed, still empty.

Happy Birthday, Stephen.

Empty Nest

I cannot scale that mountain now.
Not really.

I cannot marry
that diminutive image

so, I greet the boy for who he is
and what he was:

a still-born moment of love

conceived outside
the growing season.

Buried now
inside me

he seems in solitude
a headstone

along well-worn paths
deep inside forests

clouded over

as I wander past
a troubled mind

or sit, relaxed, treasuring
hard eyes, sweet hands

& loving bodies
we created:

two able daughters.

Another day, perhaps
I'll take his hand

and walk
uphill a mile

to unknown
lands

ignorant
of moons

of suffering,

pregnant
with its own light

that shed
understanding

on fields
of want & love

death & progeny.

Why is it so hard
dear, to express joy

when mountains
hide

green far sides
for decades

right inside me?

Echo

Hassan measures all four chambers.
Mitral flips its finger, time & time
again. Aorta I glimpse by twisting
sideways; black hole looks more
arse than gateway to brainstem.

Uncomplaining, greyscale
images float past, a bouquet
of memories, drowning. One
stops at Hassan's back door.
Blood struggles to exit, enter, all
but divorced. *End of a golf game?*

Beaten, as if on hands & knees
muscles pump fiercely, eager to
clutch vein railings, forcing blood
to climb stairs to upper chambers.
Hassan turns away as, again, I

brag, how, as a teen, I told dad
I'd always be older, born one month
earlier on the Julian calendar.
He smiles, kindly.

   Sideways, these
chambers resemble skulls—sockets
empty, mouths agape—until greyscale
gives way to blue strokes & orange
flashes. Pregnant with blood again

the old Bell pepper feeds flesh
another day. Mitral valve? Putts
every grade. All holes-in-one. Just thumps
away. *Warned him. Died on me anyway.*

Embrace

Your warm embrace of the widowed neighbor who lost
her son to cancer wakes another day to cardinals, alarmed, as
light drops off window sills, bright as dragons' blood. Faced with fear
we grow blind with tears: heads wag, hearts mutter, tongues stutter & untolled

grief unfolds in us its one true color. Yours grows crimson gold
& red—mine mottled, light as a feather. Faith, that fallen leaf, lies frozen
to the ground, forgetful of the sun. And when death comes, looking for its brother
grief wields unyielding power: we mourn in bitter sorrow to our better selves. Yet death is nothing

but the stunted butler to its own corpse. Death waits on all of us. Come
love, walk with me awhile on sacred ground. Grieve on winter's wings, if you must
but let high winds sharpen the sword's tongue. Entwine your fingers in mine. Embrace
night's bright tapestry, cold as a feudal beggar. And when the wolf-heart leaps, fangs dripping

crystalline blood, howl death's unnatural name: *Mesothelioma!* What a fit romantic grave for someone else's
lung cancer. Medieval this grief; no virgin, us, stained by widowed love.

Christmas

I neglect those Christmases now, her red unpitted heart
that thick brown hair bound up in a mourning wreath.

You say he slumbers next to you & me, in timbered thought?

More faint, yes; more brief than is the hidden heart
from whose loins this self-love grew.

Now, mostly, he gathers me to himself beside friends;
loiters at the edges, unsaid; a shape of frail speech
or passing image; then strolls away.

He retreats to everyday worlds while you—tailored
in that business dress, or me in a tan suit
drive off to work or jog past gardens
of grief, now dying.

Dear, I stand before you
outside that me, naked
in burnished love

bodies
trembling.

Thank you.

Hands clasped
may be

the last
best

fig
leaf.

Ménage à Trois

[Death, you nubile odalisque beast, go to hell or bed!]
No, dear. It's nothing. [Remember shared smiles
climbing crooked stairs beneath Paris' L *'Ossuary?*

Your sometimes face, lit the darkness, flashing
heartbeats, opened cages of blue light deep
inside my chest; red flickers meant liberty.

Well-born before we bed, I confessed I'd marry
you—you, me—and beget a bastard child. That vow
though not yet kept, too soon I'm bound to keep.

Already I fret, smell urine in sex; miss intimacy. Pounds
of flesh worn in health, now feels old lingerie, diseased.]
Yes, I'll wear the hollow crown. Reek All Hallows Eve.

That Boy, Again?

Old Friends, I fear, have taken him
to camp among beaten men. Once,
at ten, I woke among such men
afield. Back then, Reuben Young

a soldier, clutched us to his breast
enraged, whenever we'd strike a
brother with sticks. He filled our
ears with Korean names—war burnt

that hard in him; shame for taking lives.
John Cotter, too, dad's favorite Irish
hand, died much the same: hanged
himself one drunken weekend; that

and he felt worthless for being bailed
again. *Who sits at Easter table &
resurrect their sins? Not JC,* he'd
say, and, by Christ, laugh again.

But most I see—no, fail to see
one faceless man who slit both pale
wrists on dad's barbed-wire fence.
Silent he fell, at first; silent blood

swelled a dozen pine needle shells
lying next to him. Those muffled yells
sending pheasants flying wild past
frightened wind—golden browns & yellow

iridescent feathers went flying while winter's
one blood-red eye never blinked; but bodies
squawked across captive Iowa cornfields.
Trees, barren, now abandoned, windswept

& heavy with snow, heaved with wrath;
began to moan & grasp at each
other's shadows; became a stand silent
as ghosts—a froze row of metronomes.

All this, and that still-born calf
at dawn, brought to mom's kitchen:
sacrificial lives. None lived. That
dying man dragged his body

though us kids' make-believe villages,
calloused hands digging this
way & that, booted toes disturbing
pine-needle roads, collapsed

lungs lunging at one last breath,
his weighted body cold; thin
—I hold these images sacred
in avid, adolescent memory.

So, yes, dear wife, his dread, my
fears, all grow fierce at times
as a warm-breathed animal—
sometimes, for no good reason.

And I've thrown a shoe or two at it,
at death, at beasts & other fears
grown tall; but even then, some
tower over me. These feelings

live on, rise & die within.
But that boy I cannot kill
and never will
for doing so changes
nobody & nothing.

And when I go to war
he tracks me
to the cave
just down the hill
past oceans brave with light

past fields of speech
where I abandon him

or he me, on beaches that field
no horizon, utter no beams of light
—nor can we, come night, find or defend lands' end.

IV.

Epilogue

Book. Released.

Noscitur a sociis

eyes closed
words run thin
pages turn
mind drawn in

sleep draws near
dreams more dear
you go now
I stay here

Caroline Bock

Graphic Designer's Biography

Sanket Patel is an experienced 33-year-old graphic designer, illustrator, and web designer from Groton, Connecticut. He was born in India and moving to the states at age five. He developed a strong appreciation for cultures of both India and the United States. His style as an artist incorporates his Indian roots and expresses this culture it in a modern and innovative way. He has several years of experience, working in a multitude of design roles and settings, Sanket has become a very sought-after designer, and is able to bring a creative, yet professional approach to any project.

Artist's Biography

Grace Cavalieri is a poet, playwright, painter and radio host of the Library of Congress program *The Poet and the Poem*. She has published 26 books and chapbooks of poetry, plus fiction. She has written numerous produced plays, plus texts for two produced operas. In 2019, Cavalieri was appointed the tenth Poet Laureate of Maryland.

Grace holds The Association of Writers & Writing Programs' George Garrett Award, the Pen-Fiction Award, two Allen Ginsberg Poetry Awards, the Bordighera Poetry Award, the Paterson Award for Excellence, Phi Beta Kappa, and The Corporation for Public Broadcasting Silver Medal.

In 1976, Cavalieri co-founded the Washington Writers Publishing House with John McNally, then served on its editorial board to 1982. In 1979 she founded The Bunny and the Crocodile Press/Forest Woods Media Productions, Inc., a publishing house and media production company. Forest Woods Media Productions produces *The Poet and the Poem* for podcasts and public radio, now celebrating 45 years. She has produced more than 100 programs in radio drama, and poetry and arts criticism, including *Poetry from the City, Expressions,* and *Writer's Workshop on the Air.*

Anna Nicole: Poems, published in March, 2008, presents her feminist voice at its liveliest; In *LIFE UPON THE WICKED STAGE: A Memoir,* published in May 2015, she casts a telling eye across her manifold life. Recent books include *The Secret Letters of Madame de Stael* (2021), *What The Psychic Said* (2020), *Showboat* (2019), and *Other Voices, Other Lives* (2018).

Cavalieri served as an Associate Director of Programming at the Public Broadcasting System for five years and subsequently served as program officer of the National Endowment for the Humanities media program from 1982 to 1988. She has lectured and taught throughout the US at several colleges and universities, and was, for 25 years, visiting poet at St. Mary's College of Maryland. She was resident writer at the Word Works annual retreat in Tuscany, 1996–2003, and was book editor of *The Montserrat Review* until 2011. She writes a monthly poetry feature entitled "Exemplars" for the *Washington Independent Review of Books* (2011–present).

Grace Cavalieri received her BS in English Literature and History from the College of New Jersey-Trenton and an MFA in Creative Writing from Goddard University. she continued graduate studies at the University of Maryland, College Park and Rollins University in Florida.

Grace Cavalieri lives in Annapolis, Maryland.

Author's Biography

Winner of the 2019 William Meredith Award in Poetry

Photo by: Kate C. Kirlin

Tom Kirlin is the recipient of the 2019 William Meredith Award in Poetry for *Enabling Love, A Poetic Tribute* to William Meredith, the winner of the Pulitzer Prize, National Book Award and many other literary honors. Kirlin's accomplishments include the Larry Neal Award for Poetry, a grant from the District of Columbia's Commission on the Arts and a National Endowment for the Humanities fellowship for post-doctoral studies at Yale University.

Kirlin taught at the University of Wisconsin-Madison before moving to Washington, DC. Here, he worked for several decades on energy, science, environmental and technology policy issues after providing educational and writing services to professional organizations that represent artists, chemists, architects, energy groups and minority investors. During these years he helped launch and edited *The Journal of Minority Business Finance;* created a national radio program on the first personal computers; worked with NGOs during the U.N. climate negotiations that produced the 1997 Kyoto Protocols; and served as Vice President at the Center for the Study of the Presidency, a non-profit, non-partisan organization. Here, he helped revive a Fellows program and co-edited *Triumphs & Tragedies of the Modern Presidency: Seventy-Six Case Studies in Presidential Leadership.*

Kirlin honed his writing craft at Bread Loaf, a Colrain Poetry Manuscript Conference and at Tom Jenks' Narrative Workshop. Following a summer at Bread Loaf, Little Red Tree Publishing issued Tom's first book of poems, *Under the Potato Moon,* in 2013. Other poems have appeared in anthologies—*Hungry as We Are, The WPFW Poetry Anthology* and *Cabin Fever*—and in literary journals—most recently, in *Crosswinds.* A grant from the James Smithson Society enabled him and his wife to celebrate the Smithsonian Institution's 25th Folklife Festival in their co-authored *The Smithsonian Folklife Cookbook.*

Tom Kirlin and his wife, Katherine, live in Washington, DC. Kirlin recently became Secretary of the William Meredith Foundation.

www.ingramcontent.com/pod-product-compliance
Lightning Source LLC
Chambersburg PA
CBHW042247100526
44587CB00002B/46